NATIONAL AUDUBON SOCIETY
POCKET GUIDES

**National
Audubon Society**

The mission of the NATIONAL AUDUBON SOCIETY
*is to conserve and restore natural ecosystems, focusing
on birds and other wildlife for the benefit of humanity
and the Earth's biological diversity.*

We have nearly 600,000 members and an extensive
chapter network, plus a staff of scientists, lobbyists,
lawyers, policy analysts, and educators. Through our
sanctuaries we manage 150,000 acres of critical habitat.

Our award-winning *Audubon* magazine carries
outstanding articles and color photography on wildlife,
nature, and the environment. We also publish *American
Birds,* an ornithological journal, *Audubon Activist,* a
newsjournal, and *Audubon Adventures,* a newsletter
reaching 500,000 elementary school students. Our
World of Audubon television shows air on TBS and
public television.

For information about how you can become a member,
please write or call the Membership Department at:

NATIONAL AUDUBON SOCIETY
700 Broadway, New York, New York 10003
(212) 979-3000

FAMILIAR BIRDS OF SEA AND SHORE

Text by Simon Perkins

Alfred A. Knopf, New York

This is a Borzoi Book
Published by Alfred A. Knopf, Inc.

Copyright © 1994 Chanticleer Press, Inc.
All rights reserved.
Published in the United States by Alfred A. Knopf, Inc.,
New York, and simultaneously in Canada by Random House
of Canada Limited, Toronto. Distributed by Random
House, Inc., New York.

Prepared and produced by Chanticleer Press, Inc.,
New York.
Printed and bound by Dai Nippon Printing Co., Ltd., Tokyo.

Published February 1994
First Printing

Library of Congress Catalog Number: 93-21251
ISBN: 0-679-74921-7

Contents

Introduction
How to Use This Guide 6
Birdwatching 8
Identifying Birds 11
Birds of Coastal Regions 15
The Families of Birds 18

The Birds 24

Appendices
Parts of a Bird 184
Glossary 186
Index 188
Credits 191

How to Use This Guide

Birds are virtually everywhere—in cities; in forests and fields; in the middle of oceans (above and below the surface); in the center of Antarctica; and over 30,000 feet above sea level. The omnipresence of birds is one of the reasons why birdwatching has become so popular. Another reason is because birding is so simple: anyone equipped with a pair of binoculars and a bird book is ready to start.

Coverage

This guide introduces 80 of the most common species of birds encountered on the coasts and in the coastal waters of North America. They include birds that spend most of their lives at sea, such as albatrosses, shearwaters, and fulmars; a variety of gulls and terns; shorebirds like oystercatchers and sandpipers; herons and egrets; and waterfowl.

Organization

There are three parts to this guide: introductory information, illustrated species accounts, and appendices.

Introduction

This section outlines the various aspects of bird identification, with tips for beginners on basic birding techniques, optics, and other equipment. There is also a brief description of each major group of birds included in this book, with helpful commentary on bird behavior and bird family characteristics.

The Birds This main section of the guide contains color plates on 80 representative bird species, along with a description of each species' salient field marks. There is also information on voice, habitat, and range. An outline map showing the breeding and winter ranges accompanies the written range descriptions (see example at left). Where there is an overlap between breeding and winter ranges, or wherever a species occurs year-round, the crosshatching indicates the permanent range. For consistency, ranges are cut off at the Mexican border, even though many species occur south of there. Accompanying each species account is a small silhouette, designed as an aid in identification. These silhouettes represent general body types but do not necessarily indicate the subtle variations that can occur among species of the same family.

Breeding range

Winter range

Permanent range

Appendices Two labeled drawings—one of a gull and the other of a bird's wing—name the major parts of a bird that are used in identification. The Glossary further defines these and other technical terms used in this book and by birders in general. Finally, the Index lists both scientific and common names of the species covered in this guide.

Birdwatching

Birdwatching is a fast-growing and enormously popular pastime. Estimates suggest that between 60 and 80 million people are involved with birding to some extent. Standard equipment for birdwatching includes a pair of binoculars, a spotting scope, and a tripod on which to mount the scope. Most birding can be done with binoculars only, but in any situation where birds are very distant, such as seabirds on the ocean viewed from shore, a scope becomes nearly essential. The simplest way to become familiar with the best available choices in equipment is to talk with other birders to see what they use. Birders are generally a frugal lot, and will be able to tell you where to get the best values.

Binoculars
You get what you pay for with optics, and what you want to get is optical clarity and durability. Binoculars range in price from $75 to $1,200, with very acceptable binoculars available from $150 to $200. Specifications for binoculars are given in terms of two measurements. The most common combination of these two numbers is seven and thirty-five, given as 7×35. In this example, 7 represents the number of times the instrument magnifies an image, and 35 equals the diameter of each objective lens (the lenses closest to the object being viewed) in millimeters. Choose binoculars with a

magnification between seven and ten power. Anything less than $7\times$ is simply not enough, and anything more than $10\times$ becomes difficult to hold steady enough to see an image clearly. For this reason zoom binoculars are not recommended.

Spotting Scopes
Spotting scopes provide higher magnification, but must be used with a tripod or other device to provide stability. Scope prices vary, from $200 to $1000. Good tripods cost between $100 and $300. A cheaper one is likely to be flimsy and unstable, and stability is what a tripod is all about. Cheaper, but less versatile alternatives to a tripod include a small bean bag or a window mount that clamps onto a partly raised car window.

Other Equipment
Be prepared for the elements. If you live in the north in the winter, wear (or at least bring with you) more layers than you think you'll need. The coast is generally windier than interior locales, so allow for the chill factor. Knee-high rubber boots will allow you access to marshes and other wetlands in comfort, and good foul-weather gear will provide protection from rain. Birds usually remain warm, dry, and active during inclement weather. With the proper gear, you can too.

Birding Technique In some respects, birding is like a sport, and like any sport, it helps to know some basics when you're just getting started. Like the proper mechanics of a golf swing, it will help to use proper technique when birding. The use of binoculars is essential to bird identification. Get comfortable with your binoculars. Practice spotting with them. Initially, the simple act of finding a bird in your binoculars will be challenging, especially when the bird is moving. But with practice it will become second nature. When looking for a bird with your binoculars, try to raise the optics into your line of sight without moving your eyes. Before raising them, make a mental note of the image immediately around the bird (a distinctive fork in a branch; a buoy floating nearby; a tree on the horizon), and match that image (on a larger scale, of course) in the binoculars. Once you have found the bird, assume a position you can hold for a long time. Balance your weight and keep your elbows down. This stance will allow you to keep your binoculars steady.

Identifying Birds

The process of bird identification is not always easy. But when approached systematically, the task is not as daunting as it may first appear. Many different methods can be used to narrow the possibilities. Begin with the most obvious features and proceed to the finer points.

Size and Shape

Size and shape are good starting points. When determining size, use another species of known size as a frame of reference. This may take a little time, since birds often appear before us in a void (e.g., soaring in an empty sky or swimming on a large expanse of water). What about shape? Does the bird appear stocky or slim? Are the wings pointed or rounded? Narrow or broad? Is the tip of the tail squared off, pointed, or forked? When considering shape, also note features such as the proportional length of the wings, tail, legs, and bill. Study the bill shape because this often provides the best clue for placing a bird in a particular group. Be aware that birds can raise and lower their feathers much the way dogs and cats can raise and lower their fur; in so doing, they can appear to change shape. Larger birds often change wing shape as well, flexing their wings outward while soaring, or raking them back while gliding or diving. Additionally, many birds—particularly herons and egrets—can alter the apparent length of their necks, by drawing them in or stretching them out.

Season, Range, and Habitat Use the process of elimination. Once you can place a bird into a specific group, check the book to see which species within that group occurs in that part of the country, in that season, in that particular habitat. In time, you will begin to anticipate which birds to expect under various circumstances. This will allow you to significantly reduce the number of viable possibilities, and thereby make the task of identification much easier. For example, over 50 species of shorebirds occur in North America. But if you see a flock of sandpipers on rocks on the coast of Maine in January, you will find that only one species is typically found there then, under that precise set of circumstances: the Purple Sandpiper. Not all birds fit so neatly into a pattern, but the process of elimination is bound to help.

Color and Pattern Consider specific plumage characteristics. Does the plumage show any areas of contrast, or is it uniform? Is the plumage streaked (lines along the axis of the body) or barred (lines across the axis of the body)? Another caution: Light can play tricks. The angle and quality of light can dramatically alter the apparent color of a bird's plumage.

For example, midday light tends to make colors appear more washed out, while morning and evening lights infuse colors with a warm orange or reddish cast. Strong back lighting (when the light source is behind the subject) generally makes an object appear darker than normal. Keep these factors in mind when comparing a bird you've seen with its photograph. Photographs are also subject to other vagaries such as exposure and film type.

Behavior Behavior can be as useful for identification as plumage. Does the bird fly low or high? Are the wing beats slow, fast, deep, or shallow? Does it feed actively or sluggishly? Where does it feed—in mud? sand? grass? If it is a waterfowl, does it take flight abruptly, or does it run across the surface of the water before gradually taking flight? Does it dive below the surface?

Voice Virtually all North American birds can be identified by voice alone; it is just harder to learn calls because most birds give several different types of vocalizations, and written descriptions are subject to a wider range of interpretation than are visual field marks. However, several new cassette tapes now teach you what to listen for in terms of bird vocalizations. In this guide, a written description of the most commonly heard vocalization for each species is included in its respective account. However, these descriptions represent only one phonetic interpretation. Learn to apply your own characterizations to the calls as you hear them.

Gestalt   Experienced birders can often identify a bird given only the briefest glimpse at a great distance. This feat is not as magical as it sounds, however. Imagine scanning a crowd for someone you've known your entire life. You would know that person's subtle mannerisms and could recognize him or her from behind, even from a distance, just by the way he or she moved. Each bird species has its own distinctive "look," an essence created by the sum of its parts, by which, with years of practice, the species can be recognized. There is no good word in English for this look. In German it is called gestalt.

Birds of Coastal Regions

The coastal regions of North America offer a rich and varied assortment of habitats in which to see an equally rich assortment of birds. These coastal birds might be found in salt marshes and river estuaries; on sandy beaches, mud flats, or rocky headlands; or in harbors, bays, or open sea.

When and Where to Look for Birds

The birds of sea and shore generally are more abundant in spring and fall, when many species use the coast as a migratory route. But many others appear in the winter, when they move to the coast as inland water freezes. Some birds, such as sea ducks, feed together on the ocean in enormous groups called rafts. Others, such as night-herons, skulk alone through tidal creeks. Frigatebirds may spend the entire day in the air, patrolling the shoreline for a potential meal.

How to See the Birds

Obviously, the closer you approach the birds the better you can see them, and the more easily you can identify them. So learn how to get close. Birds are more sensitive to motion than they are to sound. Don't move unless you have to. Even raising a hand to scratch your head looks suspicious to a bird. When you do move, move very slowly, and keep a low profile. Some species are more wary than others, flying or scurrying away as you approach. Learn how to read the bird's state of alertness. Much of this is common sense. If a bird is keeping a constant eye on you and walking or swimming directly away, you are too close. Freeze until it resumes "normal" behavior. If it is preening, feeding, or standing on one foot, it is relaxed and not likely to flush. Practice stalking different types of birds like gulls on a beach or ducks on a pond.

Getting Closer Cars make excellent "blinds" from which to watch or photograph birds. If you wish to approach a bird or flock of birds with a car, approach slowly and, more important, stop slowly. Being still has the added benefit of allowing you to more easily detect movement around you, and there is no better way to spot birds than by their movement.

Tides The schedules of coastal birds are determined largely by tides. Loons and seaducks may be found closer to shore on a higher tide, feeding gulls and terns are often attracted to inlets on falling or rising tides, and many shorebirds feed on flats that are exposed at low tide. Most newspapers publish the times of local tide cycles.

The Lee "Lee" refers to an area protected from wind behind an object or body of land. Buffeting winds can make it difficult to hold your binoculars or a scope steady. So, on windy days, seek a lee whenever it is practical.

Weather   Get in the habit of studying local weather: it can have a significant effect on the movements of birds and their observability. Migrating birds tend to move in greatest numbers immediately following the passage of weather fronts. In North America, they travel south in fall on northerly tailwinds associated with cold fronts, and return north in the spring on southerly tailwinds associated with warm fronts. Large coastal storms sometimes sweep seabirds shoreward within sight of land. Learn to read the basic symbols on weather maps. Most daily newspapers publish such maps.

Conservation   The birds of sea and shore are among the most vulnerable of all species to human-caused threats. The continuing destruction of wetlands and the pollution of estuaries and seashores throughout the hemisphere jeopardize the nesting and wintering grounds as well as the migratory stopover points of countless species. Becoming interested in watching these unique creatures may inspire you to take part in the efforts of the National Audubon Society, and others, to protect these habitats.

17

The Families of Birds

Ornithologists place birds into distinct groups based on structural characteristics, genetic similarity, vocalizations, and behavior. In this guide, there are 14 families represented, some by only a single species. Just as the scientific names for birds are written in Latin, so too are the family names, which appear here in parentheses.

Loons and Grebes

Loons (Gaviidae) and grebes (Podicipedidae) are highly aquatic birds that superficially resemble ducks. They leave the water only when flying or nesting, and even then some species build a floating nest of aquatic vegetation. They breed almost exclusively on fresh water and migrate to the coast when fresh water freezes. Their winter plumage differs considerably from their breeding plumage.

Seabirds

The tubenoses, including albatross (Diomedeidae), shearwaters and fulmars (Procellariidae), and storm-petrels (Hydrobatidae), are among the world's most oceanic birds. They wander widely at sea and come ashore only to nest.

Gannets

Gannets (Sulidae) are very large black and white, gooselike birds that breed in large, crowded colonies on islands in the North Atlantic. They catch fish with their bills by plunging from considerable heights, head first, into the sea.

18

Pelicans	Pelicans (Pelecanidae) are enormous birds with short, thick legs, and a very large bill. An expandable throat pouch below their bill is used to scoop fish from the water.
Cormorants	Cormorants (Phalacrocoracidae) are large, blackish birds that also feed on fish. They propel themselves underwater with powerful strokes of their feet, pursuing their prey with surprising speed and agility.
Frigatebirds	Frigatebirds (Fregatidae) are very large, long-winged birds that resemble pterodactyls. They are highly aerial, spending most of their lives in flight.
Herons and Egrets	Herons and egrets (Ardeidae) are large, long-necked, long-legged waders that hunt for their aquatic food by standing still in or next to shallow water, waiting for prey to approach. Several species have pure white plumages.
Waterfowl	The waterfowl include swans, ducks, and geese (Anatidae). Most waterfowl have fairly (to very) long necks and characteristic flattened bills. Swans make use of their very long necks to reach aquatic vegetation on the bottom of shallow water bodies, tipping vertically so that their entire front end is submerged. Geese are increasingly common, feeding on land in grassy areas and cornfields or flying high

overhead in formation during migration. Ducks comprise the largest group among the waterfowl, and can be divided into two other groups: dabbling ducks, and bay and sea ducks. Dabblers generally prefer smaller, more protected bodies of water, where they feed from the surface, while the bay and sea ducks, as the names indicate, are more often found in open water, and dive for their food.

Osprey   The osprey (Accipitridae), a large, long-winged raptor, feeds almost exclusively on fish. It catches its food near the surface of the water, by means of spectacular high-dives, grasping its prey with its powerful talons as it plunges into the water.

Shorebirds   Shorebirds comprise a large and highly diverse group that includes avocets and stilts (Recurvirostridae), oystercatchers (Haematopodidae), plovers (Charadriidae), and sandpipers (Scolopacidae). All share a common affinity for coastal habitats, though some are found inland as well, especially during migration. The sandpipers are the largest group; most are mainly brownish above and paler below, and vary considerably in respect to size, bill structure, and habits.

Gulls and Terns	Gulls, terns, and jaegers (Laridae) are a large family of birds. Jaegers are the oceanic equivalent of hawks. They survive by preying upon other seabirds or harassing them until they relinquish their catch. Away from their breeding grounds they are largely oceanic. Gulls and terns inhabit virtually all coastal areas. Both feed by catching fish, but the larger gulls are more adaptable, and have learned to exploit a wider range of habitats and food types. Most terns typically plunge-dive head first into the water for their food.
Alcids	Alcids (Alcidae) are the Northern Hemisphere equivalents of penguins. They are sturdy seabirds that swim equally well above or below the surface of the water, and feed primarily on fish.
Kingfishers	Kingfishers (Alcedinidae) are aquatic relatives of the woodpeckers. They eat fish and other water-borne prey, and hunt by hovering over the water, diving head first, and grasping their prey with their bills.

THE BIRDS

Red-throated Loon *Gavia stellata*

Superbly adapted to an aquatic life, loons breed on fresh-water lakes or ponds and migrate to salt water in winter. Though all loons are similar in winter plumage, more white on the face of winter Red-throateds helps separate them from Pacific and Common loons. The slimmest of loons, Red-throateds have a thinner bill held at a slight upward angle when swimming.

Identification
24–27". In all plumages, back is dark gray finely speckled with white; underparts white. In breeding plumage, has a gray head and neck and brick-red throat-patch. In winter, has white from the top of the eye through the foreneck. Immature shows a "dirty" throat.

Voice
Seldom heard except on breeding grounds, where it utters wails, shrieks, and low growl.

Habitat
Tundra and coastal lakes and ponds in summer; coastal bays and estuaries in winter.

Range
Arctic south to Manitoba and Newfoundland; winters along Atlantic and Pacific coasts, rare on Great Lakes.

Common Loon *Gavia immer*

This large black and white water bird is well-known as a symbol of wilderness. Henry David Thoreau described an encounter with a Common Loon on Walden Pond: Out in his canoe, the Concord author spotted a loon and determined to chase it. Thoreau was repeatedly confounded, however, as the loon dove and reappeared in yet another location, signaling its escape with a hearty "loon-laugh."

Identification 28–36". Large, heavy daggerlike bill. Breeding plumage shows black head and neck with a white necklace. Back is checkered black and white; underparts are white. Winter plumage is dark gray above, white below.

Voice A loud, laughing yodel and a mournful wail, often heard at night on its breeding territory.

Habitat Large, forested lakes with many small islands; oceans and bays in winter.

Range Breeds primarily in the North, from Alaska east through northern Canada and in northern forested states. Winters on all coasts.

Horned Grebe *Podiceps auritus*

The Horned Grebe leads a double life. Its outward appearance and chosen habitat differ so radically in summer and winter that one might think it two different species. During summer this gaily feathered bird resides on inland, freshwater wetlands; with the arrival of winter, however, its plumage becomes muted and the bird moves to salt water.

Identification 12–15". A small ducklike bird always found in water. In summer, note the rusty-red foreneck and flanks as well as the golden-buff ear-tufts. In winter, dark gray above and white below; the white extends up onto the cheek, in contrast to darker side of the head on the Eared Grebe.

Voice Loud shrieks, and chatters that sound like a tape recording on fast forward.

Habitat Lakes and marshes with open water in summer; winters mostly on salt water and also on the Great Lakes.

Range Breeds from Alaska and northern Canada south to Great Lakes. Winters along coasts.

Eared Grebe *Podiceps nigricollis*

This gregarious waterbird nests in large colonies and collects in huge rafts (flocks) on its wintering quarters. Over a million congregate each winter on the Salton Sea in southern California. Its diet consists primarily of small fish, crustaceans, and aquatic insect larvae. When frightened, grebes sometimes sink slowly into the water, leaving only their heads exposed.

Identification
: 12–14". Breeding plumage is dark brown and blackish with rusty flanks and straw-colored ear-tufts extending back from eye. Black head is crested. In winter, limited white on the upper throat, chin, and behind the ear; underparts are white. White patches in wing are visible in flight.

Voice
: Usually silent, except on breeding grounds, where it utters froglike peeps and squeaky whines.

Habitat
: Breeds in marshy freshwater lakes and ponds; winters on open freshwater lakes and in saltwater bays.

Range
: Breeds inland from British Columbia and Manitoba south to California and Texas. Winters along the Pacific and Gulf coasts, occasionally east to Florida panhandle.

30

Western Grebe *Aechmophorus occidentalis*

A graceful long-necked diving bird, the Western Grebe is known for its "dancing-on-water" courtship display. It breeds on western lakes and winters along the Pacific coast. Western is distinguished from very similar Clark's Grebe by black head markings that extend below the eye, giving a mask effect. Clark's black cap does not reach the eye.

Identification 22–29". Large grebe, resembling a loon. Overall black and white with a long, thin yellowish-green bill. The bill of Clark's Grebe is yellowish orange.

Voice A repeated *crick crick!,* the tone like that of a cricket, but less measured.

Habitat Nests in large, freshwater lakes with reeds and rushes. Winters along coastal shores, bays, and large inland lakes.

Range Breeds from central Canada south to New Mexico, west to the Pacific coast. Winters mainly along the Pacific coast with some birds along the Gulf Coast east to Alabama; rarely to the East Coast.

Black-footed Albatross *Diomedea nigripes*

Among all birds, albatrosses are perhaps the most superbly adapted to life at sea. Huge birds with enormous wingspans (the largest, the Wandering Albatross, has a wingspan of almost 11 feet), they are capable of covering vast expanses of open ocean in search of food. The Black-footed Albatross nests on several mid-Pacific islands including several in the Hawaiian archipelago, and visits the waters off the West Coast with greater frequency than any other albatross species.

Identification 28–36". Huge. Dark sooty brown with a pale face and belly. The bird has extremely long, narrow wings.

Voice Screeches and grunts. During courtship, issues a variety of bill-clapping noises, whistles, and quacks.

Habitat Open ocean; rarely seen from shore.

Range Breeds on mid-Pacific islands, including Hawaiian Islands. Ranges along the entire Pacific coast of North America.

Northern Fulmar *Fulmarus glacialis*

This northern seabird often follows fishing vessels, and scavenges fish whenever possible. Fulmars and their relatives share a keen sense of smell, a trait rather rare among birds, and can locate food from great distances by following a scent plume upwind over the surface of the ocean.

Identification 17–20". Highly variable, ranging in appearance from very pale gray and white (light morph) to uniformly medium gray (dark morph), or any mottled combination in between. Light morph is similar in basic pattern to the adult Herring Gull, but in any plumage is easily told by shorter, much narrower wings and characteristic shearwater-like flight. Told from shearwaters by coloration and stockier build.

Voice Usually silent; utters grunts and cackles in feeding flocks.

Habitat Open ocean; nests colonially on seaside cliffs.

Range Circumpolar breeder in North Atlantic, North Pacific, and adjacent Arctic seas. Winters in North Atlantic roughly as far south as New England; in the Pacific, south to Baja California.

36

Greater Shearwater *Puffinus gravis*

The Greater Shearwater nests on a small group of oceanic islands in the South Atlantic. But despite their limited nesting range, the birds disperse widely into the North Atlantic following breeding, where they become the most common shearwater. Its distinctive black cap and white rump help separate Greater from Cory's Shearwater.

Identification   18–20". Typical shearwater flight includes gliding very low over the water with occasional quick, stiff wingbeats and steeply banked, high arcing turns. Blackish-brown upperparts interrupted only by a white collar and rump. Underparts largely white with dark mottling on underwing and rarely seen blackish smudge on belly. Clean black cap on otherwise white head separates Greater from Cory's, which shows dusky crown blending into white on face.

Voice   Usually silent except when resting in flocks on the water.

Habitat   Open ocean; nests on oceanic islands.

Range   Nests on oceanic islands in the South Atlantic. In the spring and summer, migrates into the North Atlantic as far north as Labrador.

Sooty Shearwater *Puffinus griseus*

Shearwaters are named for their habit of occasionally
grazing the surface of the sea with a wing tip as they bank
and turn low over the water. Hundreds of thousands of
Sooty Shearwaters may be seen off the Pacific Northwest
coast, streaming by during migration. In the Atlantic, they
are not so abundant. The Short-tailed Shearwater, a smaller
look-alike that occurs among flocks of Sooties in the Pacific,
has a slightly darker underwing.

Identification 16–18". Dark ash-gray overall with silvery underwings.
Wings long and narrow. Typical shearwater flight, fast and
graceful, gliding low over the water with occasional quick,
snappy wingbeats and steeply banked, high arcing turns.

Voice Usually silent except for a variety of cooing and croaking
notes heard on the breeding grounds.

Habitat Open ocean.

Range Breeds in the South Pacific and winters (during our
summer) in North American waters along both coasts.
Nests on islands off South America, New Zealand, and
Australia; migrates along Atlantic and Pacific coasts.

40

Wilson's Storm-Petrel *Oceanites oceanicus*

Despite its diminutive size, this seabird is remarkably hardy, capable of enduring raging storms over the open ocean, where it spends most of its life. Scarcely larger than a swallow, it deftly avoids the brunt of gales by remaining in the troughs of the waves where the strength of the wind is diminished. When feeding, Wilson's Storm-Petrel appears to walk on the water, pattering its feet as it flutters over the surface searching for tiny scraps of fish or plankton.

Identification 7". Tiny. Erratic, fluttery flight low over surface of water. Uniformly blackish brown except for bold white rump-patch that wraps around side of rump onto vent. Indistinct pale bar on inner wing. Very similar Leach's Storm-Petrel is longer-winged with less extensive white rump patch.

Voice A soft peeping when feeding, heard only at close range.

Habitat Open ocean.

Range Breeds on oceanic islands around Antarctica; common off Atlantic coast from May to September, a very rare visitor off the California and Gulf coasts.

42

Northern Gannet *Morus bassanus*

These large seabirds are denizens of the North Atlantic. During breeding season they occupy enormous, crowded colonies on inaccessible, rocky islands, and range out to sea to forage on shoals of fish. Thousands of individuals may congregate over schools of fish, circling high above the water until the fish approach the surface. When their quarry reach striking depth, the birds plunge headfirst into the water, sometimes from heights of over a hundred feet, to capture the fish with their bills.

Identification 35–40". Very large with long pointed bill and long pointed tail that creates a double-ended look. Adult is gleaming white with a straw-yellow head and black wing tips. Immature is dark brown. Adolescent shows variable combinations of brown and white.

Voice Usually silent; hoarse croaks or grunts when breeding.

Habitat Breeds in large colonies on rocky coastal islands.

Range Breeds in Gulf of Saint Lawrence and in Newfoundland. Winters along the Eastern Seaboard south into the Gulf of Mexico.

Brown Pelican *Pelecanus occidentalis*

Pelicans have an enormous bill and expandable throat pouch with which they so adeptly catch fish. Unlike other pelicans, the Brown Pelican captures its prey by way of a spectacular head-first dive into the water from considerable height. In flight pelicans seem to defy their bulk, soaring to great heights or gliding in formation low over the water, with their down-bowed wings nearly grazing the surface.

Identification   42–54". Very large and heavy-bodied. Long, heavy bill is usually held downward along the neck. Very short, thick legs. Largely gray-brown. Adult has a variably white to straw-yellow head with a dark brown nape and hindneck. Immature has a dark head; paler underparts.

Voice   Adults are silent; young birds in the nesting colonies are very noisy, uttering loud grunts and screams.

Habitat   Coastal waters, beaches, bays; breeds on islands in colonies.

Range   Breeds from central California to Baja California, from North Carolina south to Florida and along the Gulf Coast. Slowly expanding range northward on East Coast.

Great Cormorant *Phalacrocorax carbo*

This large blackish bird sits upright on a conspicuous perch, drying its outstretched wings as is typical of most cormorants. But unlike the Double-crested Cormorant—the only other cormorant with which it shares its range—the Great is found almost exclusively on the coast. And because the Double-crested migrates farther south, virtually any cormorant north of New Hampshire in winter is a Great.

Identification 36". Very large. Heavy bill hooked at the tip. Adult is entirely black with traces of iridescence. Bare skin around chin is orange. Throat whitish. Breeding plumage, white patch on lower flank sometimes concealed by folded wing; variable amount of fine white streaking on the head. Winter plumage lacks white head streaks and flank patch. Immature is dark brown above, pale below with a whitish belly; darker on the breast and neck.

Voice Deep, guttural grunts.

Habitat Rocky shores, coastal islands, seaside cliffs.

Range Breeds locally from northeastern Canada to Maine. Winters along the Atlantic coast, occasionally as far south as Florida.

48

Double-crested Cormorant *Phalacrocorax auritus*

The Double-crested Cormorant is the most widespread species in its family and seems to be increasing in numbers in most of its range. Cormorants spend much of their time fishing under water and their typical pose—spread-winged on a piling or buoy—indicates their need to dry their not-quite-waterproof feathers. While never domesticated, various species have assisted humans. Historically, these birds have been used by fishermen to help catch fish.

Identification 30–36". Large. Adult is entirely black with orange throat patch. Immature is dark brown above, paler below. Buff white on neck and breast, duskier on belly. (Pattern is reversed in immature Great Cormorant.) Hooked bill is held tilted slightly upward when swimming. Often migrates in large V-shaped skeins.

Voice Usually silent, except for grunts in the breeding colony.

Habitat Found on virtually any large body of water, fresh or salt.

Range Widespread breeder in North America; winters primarily along coasts, north to New Hampshire. Occasionally inland on large lakes and rivers, particularly in south.

Brandt's Cormorant *Phalacrocorax penicillatus*

Named after a nineteenth-century German zoologist, Brandt's Cormorant is the largest of the West Coast cormorants. It is especially gregarious, breeding in very large colonies where a pair's territory may be an area only as large as the space needed to land and build a nest. They also congregate in large feeding rafts where they dive for fish, generally in shallower water, closer to land than other cormorants in their range. Brandt's Cormorant has never been known to stray inland.

Identification	28–31". Large, blackish, heavy-bodied seabird with upright posture when perched on land. Short, thick, legs. Adult is blackish with pale yellow and blue throat, unique among North American cormorants. Immature is paler below.
Voice	Usually silent, except for grunts and croaks on breeding grounds.
Habitat	Nests in colonies on rocky headlands or islands.
Range	Along the Pacific coast from British Columbia to Baja California.

Pelagic Cormorant *Phalacrocorax pelagicus*

This is the smallest cormorant on the West Coast. Its small head and slender neck and bill help separate it from its larger relatives. Found primarily along the most rugged and exposed stretches of coastline, it is at home fishing in turbulent surf. Being lighter-bodied than other cormorants, it does not struggle to get airborne as others do, occasionally launching directly into the air upon surfacing from a dive.

Identification 25–30". Small and slim with a small head, slender neck, and dark, thin bill. Adult is glossy black with a small white patch on the lower flank and has a red face (less extensive than Red-faced Cormorant of Alaska). Immature is uniformly dark brown.

Voice Groaning and hissing notes around the breeding colonies.

Habitat Bays, seaside cliffs and islands, rocky shores, coastal waters. Feeds coastally or at sea.

Range Year-round, coastal resident of Pacific coast from Alaska to Baja California.

Magnificent Frigatebird *Fregata magnificens*

Frigatebirds resemble pterodactals, prehistoric flying reptiles. Their seven-foot wing spans and long forked tails make them unmistakable. The name is derived from their piratic habit of stealing fish from other seabirds, a behavior they exhibit frequently with astonishing ease and agility, even when pursuing smaller, more maneuverable victims.

Identification
37–45". Long, narrow, pointed wings held bent in flight. Long, deeply forked tail. Long bill with pronounced hook at tip. Adult male is entirely black except for inflatable red throat pouch expanded only near breeding colony. Female has white breast. Immature has white head and breast.

Voice
Generally silent except during courtship when male utters a quavering warbled call to attract the female to nest.

Habitat
Primarily aerial; often soars to great heights. Nests on islands, usually in shrubbery but sometimes on the ground.

Range
Breeds in Florida Keys. In summer, regularly wanders north along Atlantic coast to Cape Hatteras, west throughout Gulf of Mexico, and north on Pacific coast to southern California. Occasionally in Salton Sea.

Great Blue Heron *Ardea herodias*

While many heron species prefer to nest at coastal locales, the Great Blue Heron is regularly found in nesting colonies inland. A typical colony is located in the dead trees of a beaver pond and may comprise a dozen or more breeding pairs. Great Blue Herons, like most herons, are primarily fish-eaters. However, the Great Blue's more diverse diet includes mice, small birds, frogs, and other small animals that stray within striking range.

Identification 42–52". An enormous, long-legged, long-necked bird often appearing bluish-gray overall. Often called a "crane." (Cranes fly with neck outstretched; herons fly with neck folded back on itself.) Great White Heron of the Florida Keys, an all-white form of the Great Blue, is distinguished from Great Egret by pale legs (egret's legs are black).

Voice Usually silent, but emits a loud, hoarse *crak,* particularly when startled or about to take off.

Habitat Nests in tall trees. During migration and winter, in virtually any salt- or freshwater wetlands.

Range Widespread in North America south of the Arctic.

Great Egret *Casmerodius albus*

Formerly a southern species, the Great Egret, like several other heron species, has extended its breeding range northward. Nearly as large as the Great Blue Heron, it is occasionally mistaken for the white form of Great Blue (Great White Heron), which is found in south Florida.

Identification 37–41". A very large, long-necked white bird with a yellow bill and long black legs and feet. Smaller Cattle Egret has shorter neck and bill, and Great White Heron has dull yellowish legs. Smaller Snowy Egret and immature Little Blue Heron have darker bills.

Voice A deep, creaky croak.

Habitat Wooded swamps, marshy ponds and lakeshores, and fresh and salt marshes. Nests in trees or marsh shrubs near the water.

Range Summers from Oregon south to Arizona, along the Gulf Coast, and from the Great Lakes east to Maine, south to Texas and Florida. Winters in southern California, and along the southern Atlantic and Gulf coasts.

Snowy Egret *Egretta thula*

In the late nineteenth century, this small white heron was being killed by the thousands to supply the fashion trade with plumes. The Massachusetts Audubon Society, the first Audubon society, founded in 1896, was originally established in reaction to the massive plume trade. Eventually, the market's demand diminished, the plume trade was curtailed, and the bird's populations rebounded.

Identification 20–27". A medium-size egret, having entirely white plumage with a black bill, yellow facial skin, long black legs, and yellow feet. Young birds have dull greenish-yellow feet.

Voice A hoarse croak.

Habitat Nests in low vegetation in freshwater or coastal habitats; prefers a variety of wetland habitats in winter and during migration.

Range Breeds in western U.S. from Idaho south to Texas, west to California, throughout Gulf Coast, and on the East Coast north to Maine. Winters in California, along Gulf Coast, and along Atlantic coast north to Virginia.

Little Blue Heron *Egretta caerulea*

The fact that many birds undergo significant plumage changes as they mature creates a major obstacle to successful bird identification. The Little Blue Heron's striking changes during maturation provide an example. As an immature, the Little Blue is largely white, regularly confused with Snowy and Great egrets. As the Little Blue molts into adult plumage, it takes on a mottled black-and-white look that is distinctive but potentially confusing.

Identification 25–30". A medium-size heron. Adults are all dark, slate gray with deep purplish head and neck feathers, dusky greenish-gray legs, and a gray bill with a black tip. Immature is white with dull greenish-gray legs and a bicolored bill like adult.

Voice Generally silent. Occasional croaks or squawks.

Habitat Ponds, swamps, and freshwater and salt marshes. Nests colonially in trees.

Range Breeds on Atlantic coast as far north as Maine, on the Gulf Coast to Texas, and inland as far north and west as Oklahoma. In winter, withdraws from much of inland range. On East Coast, winters north to Virginia.

64

Tricolored Heron *Egretta tricolor*

The Tricolored Heron is a slender wader of salt- and freshwater coastal marshes. Because the breeding plumes, or "aigrettes," on this species are mostly dark, they were not valued as much in the plume trade. Therefore, the Tricolored Heron did not suffer severe declines during the nineteenth century. Beginning in the 1950s, the Tricolored began expanding its breeding range northward, and today occasionally nests as far north as Maine.

Identification	24–28". Slightly slimmer than most other herons and egrets, adult is mostly dark blue-gray above and white below, including foreneck and throat. Immature is similar except with dark portions of head, and neck of mostly rusty brown.
Voice	Guttural squawks and croaks.
Habitat	Salt marshes, coastal lagoons, and freshwater marshes and swamps near the coast.
Range	Breeds along coast between Texas and Florida, and from Florida north to New Jersey, occasionally to Maine. Winters throughout its breeding range, north on the Atlantic coast to Virginia.

Black-crowned Night-Heron *Nycticorax nycticorax*

During daylight hours the Black-crowned Night-Heron occupies a community roost. As dusk approaches, this stocky, short-legged bird leaves the roost and feeds in fresh- and saltwater wetlands. In areas with a variety of herons it is sometimes possible to witness a spectacular "changing of the guard" as the night-herons move out to feed and the diurnal herons return to their nocturnal roosts.

Identification 23–28". A crow-size heron, overall black and white. Note the black crown and back as well as the white underparts. Juvenile is largely brown with white spotting above and brown streaks below.

Voice Flight call is a harsh *quawk!* often heard at dusk or at night.

Habitat Wooded swamps, marshes, pond and stream edges, and a wide variety of coastal habitats, especially salt marsh, and including jetties and beaches on the open ocean.

Range Breeding range is widespread throughout contiguous 48 states and southern Canada. Found year-round in California, along the Gulf Coast, and on the Atlantic coast north to New England.

Mute Swan *Cygnus olor*

While North America has two native swans—the Tundra and Trumpeter swans—the Mute Swan is an introduced species. Mute Swans were brought from Europe over a century ago. Like other introduced species, the naturalized swans are a mixed blessing. Because they require, and are able to defend, large nesting territories, they often prevent native waterfowl from nesting in traditional locales. The Mute Swan has even been known to attack unsuspecting humans. Despite their name, Mute Swans do vocalize.

Identification 58–60". A very large, white bird with a wingspan to 8 feet. Note the orange bill and black knob below the forehead. When Mute Swans are at rest, note the downward tilt to the head and the S-shaped neck.

Voice Generally silent; hisses and grunts. Also issues a loud trumpeting call that is rarely heard.

Habitat Ponds, coastal lagoons, estuaries, and open marshes.

Range From New England south to New Jersey, and around the Great Lakes. East Coast population is slowly spreading.

70

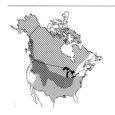

Canada Goose *Branta canadensis*

The Canada Goose is common throughout much of the United States. On migration, V-shaped skeins of these geese travel between nesting and wintering grounds, often with clamorous honking. Canada Geese are also seen roosting on ponds and lakes or grazing in fields. They regularly frequent golf courses and public parks. While most Canada Geese look alike in any given region, there is considerable size variation among the 12 geographic races.

Identification 22–45". A large waterfowl with a distinctive long black neck and head, and white cheeks and throat. The body is dark brown above, paler below.

Voice A loud, two-noted honk, the second note higher in pitch than the first.

Habitat Found in virtually any wetland situation including, occasionally, open ocean; also feeds in cornfields and is often seen grazing on short grass on golf courses and along highway median strips.

Range Virtually throughout North America.

American Black Duck *Anas rubripes*

Though not really black, the American Black Duck (shown on right) has brown plumage that appears so from a distance. A recent decline in populations is tied to several factors including ingestion of spent lead from hunting shot in feeding areas, contamination from pesticides and other toxins, and loss of critical coastal wetland nesting habitat.

Identification 19–22". Overall dark brown with a paler face and neck. The male's bill is yellow, the female's greenish yellow. In flight, note the purple speculum and silvery wing linings.

Voice Female gives a quintessential duck "quack"; male utters a quieter, hoarser rendition.

Habitat Breeds in fresh- and saltwater marshes, ponds, swamps, and lakes. In winter, it is the most common duck in most coastal salt marshes.

Range Eastern half of North America; breeds from Saskatchewan east to Prince Edward Island, south to New York, except coastally to North Carolina; winters from Canadian Maritimes and Great Lakes south to the Gulf Coast and northern Florida.

74

Greater Scaup *Aythya marila*

Known colloquially as the "Broadbill" or "Bluebill," this species and its slightly smaller relative, the Lesser Scaup, present one of the most difficult identification problems among the ducks. Away from its breeding quarters, scaup are usually found in large flocks on lakes or in bays and harbors. In winter, the Greater prefers salt water.

Identification   15½–20". Male has finely barred gray back, black breast, white sides, and iridescent blackish-green head. Bill is pale blue. Female is dark brown with white on face around base of bill. Immature male looks like female. Greater has dark greenish iridescence on rounder head, and white stripe along length of wing onto primaries. In Lesser Scaup, white in wing is only on secondaries.

Voice   Common call a loud *scaup;* females give a low *arr.*

Habitat   Lakes, bays, rivers, and tundra ponds. Winters on seacoasts and large lakes.

Range   Breeds in Alaska and northern Canada south to Ontario. Winters on the East and West coasts, the Great Lakes, and less commonly in the Mississippi Valley.

Common Eider *Somateria mollissima*

This largest of sea ducks is best known as a source of feathers for down parkas. Though all birds have down feathers, duck down is particularly thick and eider down is the most insulative. In winter, especially in New England waters, flocks of Common Eiders form immense feeding rafts as the birds dive to submarine shellfish beds. Eiders typically migrate in long undulating lines, low over water.

Identification 23–27". Heavy-bodied. Relatively long, heavy bill imparts "roman nose" profile. Adult male has white back and breast, with black sides, tail and crown. Rest of head is white with a greenish tinge visible only at close range. Female is uniformly brown, varying in tone from either grayish brown to warm cinnamon brown. Immature male is variably black and white.

Voice Courting male utters a pigeon-like cooing or moaning; female utters a grating *gog-gog-gog.*

Habitat Seacoasts.

Range Breeds along Arctic coasts; winters along the northern Atlantic and northern Pacific coasts.

Harlequin Duck *Histrionicus histrionicus*

This unique little duck is considered by many birdwatchers to be the most beautiful species of duck in North America. Exquisitely attired in a bold combination of steel-gray, black, white, and rich chestnut, these hardy birds spend their winters swimming and diving effortlessly among the rocks along surf-pounded shores.

Identification 14½–21". Adult male is unmistakable: steel-gray with bold slashes of black and white, a chestnut stripe over eye, and a broad swath of chestnut along flank. Female and immature male are dark brown with two white spots on the side of the face. Smaller overall than female scoters with much smaller bill. Female Bufflehead has one white head spot.

Voice Male emits high, squealing sounds; female, a harsh croak.

Habitat Turbulent streams and rivers in summer, exposed rocky seashores in winter.

Range Breeds in the West from Alaska south to Wyoming, and in the East from the Arctic to northern Quebec. Winters along the northern Pacific and northern Atlantic coasts.

Oldsquaw *Clangula hyemalis*

This sleek sea duck is not only one of the fastest of all ducks in flight, it is also one of the deepest divers. While foraging for shellfish it may dive to at least two hundred feet. Its far-carrying, distinctive call for which it is named is thought to have reminded early American ornithologists of women's voices.

Identification 19–22½". Male plumage is combination of brown, black, and white; whiter in winter and darker brown in summer. Other than the male Northern Pintail, this is the only duck with very long, narrow tail feathers. Female plumage has variable combinations of dark brown and white, but has a light head with a distinctive dark cheek-patch; female's tail is shorter than male's.

Voice A nasal, irregularly paced *ow-ow-owdle-LEE* rising in pitch and volume; often heard in chorus.

Habitat Tundra ponds and marshes in summer, coastal shoals in winter.

Range Breeds throughout the Arctic. Winters in coastal waters of the North Atlantic and North Pacific.

Black Scoter *Melanitta nigra*

The male of this species is the only all-black duck in North America. A bright yellow-orange, fleshy protuberance at the base of the drake's bill gives it the colloquial names used by hunters such as "Butterbill," "Yellowbill," or "Yellownose." The Black Scoter is slightly smaller and lighter-bodied than the other two scoter species, and it takes flight from the surface of the water with less effort.

Identification | 17–20½". Male is entirely black with bright yellow-orange knob at base of black bill. Female is dark brown with a pale cheek patch and a light belly. Immature male looks like the female but with a poorly developed, pale yellow knob at the base of the bill. In all plumages, the under-surface of the flight feathers is silvery.

Voice | The male may utter whistle in courtship; *cour-loo.*

Habitat | Tundra lakes and rivers in summer; along seacoasts in winter.

Range | In North America, breeds in western Alaska and northeastern Canada. Winters on both coasts.

Surf Scoter *Melanitta perspicillata*

This attractive sea duck is known by the less attractive colloquial name of "Skunk-head," for its distinctive black-and-white head pattern. Owing to the shape of the primaries, the wings of Surf Scoters produce a whistling sound in flight, similar to that produced by the wings of the Common Goldeneye.

Identification 17–21". Male plumage is black with white patches on forehead and nape; heavy, triangular bill of bright red, orange, and white; eyes white. Female is dark brown with pale belly and two whitish patches on side of head (see female White-winged Scoter). Immature male resembles female; acquires a trace of adult head and bill pattern by the first winter.

Voice Usually silent but will utter croaks and other grunting notes. In courtship, male utters a whistling call.

Habitat Tundra and forest bogs in summer; coastal during winter.

Range Breeds from Alaska throughout northern Canada to Newfoundland. Winters along both coasts; rare visitor to Gulf of Mexico.

White-winged Scoter *Melanitta fusca*

Largest of the three scoter species, the White-winged is easily distinguished from other scoters in flight by the large white patches in its secondaries. Like most sea ducks, White-wingeds subsist primarily on shellfish, which they pluck off the ocean floor with their stout bills and swallow whole. Their extraordinarily powerful gizzards are capable of crushing even the hardest shells, such as littleneck clams.

Identification | 19–23½". Heavy-bodied. Male is black with conspicuous white patches in secondaries visible at considerable distance. At closer range, exhibits a small white patch around eye. Bill is orange with a black knob at base. Female is dark brown with white wing patches as in male and two whitish patches on side of head. Not safely separable from female Surf Scoter unless the wing patches are visible.

Voice | A hoarse croak.

Habitat | Boreal forest and tundra bogs and ponds in summer; seacoasts in winter.

Range | Breeds in Alaska and western Canada; winters along both coasts.

Common Goldeneye *Bucephala clangula*

In flight, the wings of this handsome duck produce a loud whistling sound that gives rise to the species' nickname, "Whistler." Even at rest, the drake's bold black-and-white plumage renders the bird conspicuous. This species is one of the few ducks that nests in abandoned woodpecker holes in trees.

Identification 16–20". Bright yellow eye visible at close range. Male is mostly bright white with black back and dark, iridescent green head. Bold circular white patch on face forward of eye. Female and immature male are mostly gray with paler belly and dark brown head. Large white wing patches on inner half of wing are visible in flight.

Voice Courting male produces a shrill *jeee-ep;* female a low quack.

Habitat Summers on lakes and bogs in coniferous forests; winters on coastal harbors and bays as well as inland waters.

Range Breeds from Alaska throughout Canada to Newfoundland and the northern U.S. Winters in the U.S. on any open water, mostly coastally.

90

Bufflehead *Bucephala albeola*

This dapper little bird is the smallest duck in North America. Its disproportionally large head gives rise to its common name, derived from its genus, meaning "buffalo headed." Like its larger relative the Common Goldeneye, the Bufflehead nests in abandoned woodpecker holes in trees.

Identification 13–15½". Very small with a proportionally large head. Male is bold black and white. Dark iridescent green-and-purple head with broad triangular white patch extending back from the eye across nape. Back is black, rest of body is white. Female and immature male are dark brown with white spot on side of head behind the eye.

Voice Male gives a squeaky whistle; female, a low quack.

Habitat Boreal forest near small lakes and ponds in summer. Saltwater bays and harbors in winter; also lakes and rivers.

Range Breeds from central Alaska, throughout Canada to Quebec, and in the U.S. in Washington, Idaho, Montana, and Wyoming. Winters along all three coasts and inland U.S., except central mountain states.

Red-breasted Merganser *Mergus serrator*

If ducks are best defined by their bills, then mergansers are the least ducklike of all ducks. One of three species of mergansers in North America, the Red-breasted shares with its two relatives a long serrated bill superbly adapted for catching fish. The Red-breasted differs in being almost exclusively marine when away from its breeding grounds.

Identification 19½-26". Long, narrow, bright red bill. Adult male has black back, gray sides, reddish-brown speckled breast and white collar. Dark iridescent green head with wispy crest extending backward. Female and immature male have largely grayish-brown body and crested, rusty-brown head. In all plumages, white on inner half of wing visible in flight.

Voice On breeding grounds, males utter a soft *yeow-yeow*; females give a harsh *karrr*.

Habitat Lakes, rivers and, occasionally, sheltered coasts in summer; usually winters coastally on salt water.

Range Breeds from Alaska east throughout northern Canada as far south as the Great Lakes; winters along all three coasts.

Osprey *Pandion haliaetus*

This large long-winged "Fish Hawk" is, once again, a common sight along most of our shorelines. During the 1950s and 1970s it suffered severe population declines owing to contamination by DDT and other related pesticides. Since the mid-1970s, when use of DDT in the U.S. was banned, Ospreys have staged a successful comeback.

Identification   21–24". A large brown (may appear black) and white bird, often seen hovering and fishing over water. From below look for the Osprey's long, crooked wings with a dark wrist patch. Note the dark, masklike line through the eye.

Voice   A loud, repeated whistle, *kyew.*

Habitat   Wetland habitats, especially estuaries and coastal marshes as well as lakes and rivers.

Range   Breeds from Alaska east to Newfoundland, south to Arizona in the West, the Great Lakes in the Midwest, and along the entire eastern seaboard and Gulf Coast. Winters from southern Florida west along the Gulf Coast and in southern California.

Black-bellied Plover *Pluvialis squatarola*

Commonly found on expansive sand or mud flats, Black-bellieds feed like most plover species: They run a short distance, pause for a moment and glance down in search of food, run again, and so on. Black-bellieds typically appear to be quite restless and frequently advertise their presence with their far-carrying, plaintive call. They are the largest of all the North American plovers.

Identification 10½–13½". Nearly pigeon-size. Breeding plumage brightly speckled black and white above. Black below from face down to legs. White below from legs back through undertail. Winter plumage is duller, speckled black and white above and white below. In flight, note black "armpits."

Voice A clear, high-pitched, plaintive whistle: *peeoeee.*

Habitat Breeds on tundra; during migration, usually seen coastally on sand flats and marshes; less commonly on freshwater lakeshores and plowed fields.

Range Breeds in high Arctic from Alaska to Baffin Island. Winters along all three coasts from British Columbia and Massachusetts south.

98

Semipalmated Plover *Charadrius semipalmatus*

This small shorebird resembles a dark-backed Piping Plover. Like all plovers, the Semipalmated has a short bill and very sharp eyes, which serve it well while foraging for worms and other mud-dwelling invertebrates. "Palmation" is webbing between the toes; Semipalms have partial webbing between the base of their toes, hence the name.

Identification | 6½–7½". Dark gray-brown above, white below. Black mask. White from underparts extends in collar around back of neck. Single black band across breast, sometimes incomplete in winter plumage. Short, black bill is orange at the base. Legs are dull to bright orange.

Voice | A slightly squeaky, up-slurred whistle: *chu-weet.*

Habitat | Nests in gravelly areas. During migration and winter, beaches, tidal flats, shallow salt marshes, lakeshores, and, occasionally, wet fields.

Range | Breeds from Alaska across northern Canada to Newfoundland and Nova Scotia, migrating throughout the continent. Winters along all three coasts from South Carolina and California south.

100

Piping Plover *Charadrius melodus*

The Piping Plover has been placed on a federal list of threatened animals. This means that, if present trends continue, the species will continue to decline and soon face extinction. The greatest threat facing Piping Plovers is disturbance of their breeding cycle from human activity on the beaches where they nest. Some areas have been set aside as protected nesting sites, but disturbances continue.

Identification 7¼". Small, pale shorebird with short bill. Breeding plumage, upperparts very pale sand-colored, underparts white. Black collar across breast and black patch on forehead. Collar is incomplete in some individuals. Bill is orange with black tip. Legs are orange. In winter plumage, lacks black markings, bill is dark.

Voice A clear, plaintive *peep* or *peep-lo.*

Habitat Sandy beaches and dunes.

Range Breeds from Quebec and Newfoundland south to North Carolina and locally from central Alberta to Minnesota and around Great Lakes. Year-round on the Atlantic and Gulf coasts from North Carolina to Texas.

American Oystercatcher *Haematopus palliatus*

This striking shorebird is difficult to confuse with any other bird in its range. Its unique, brilliant reddish-orange, laterally compressed bill is used to pry shellfish from rocks and to extract these mollusks from their protective shells. Oystercatchers also probe in mud for invertebrates. In flight, the black-and-white wing pattern is prominent.

Identification 17–21". Unmistakable. Stocky, essentially black-and-white shorebird with long, vivid reddish-orange bill; thick, flesh-colored legs; yellow eyes. Immature is browner above with dusky tip to bill that brightens with age in first year.

Voice A piercing, slightly nasal *wheeop*. During courtship display, an excited, prolonged series of similar, shorter piping notes, often in chorus of two or more birds.

Habitat Variety of coastal habitats, including gravel beaches, exposed shellfish beds, jetties; occasionally mudflats. Breeds primarily at the upper margins of sandy beaches.

Range Year-round along the Atlantic and Gulf coasts from Delaware to Texas. Breeds on the Atlantic coast as far north as Boston.

104

Black Oystercatcher *Haematopus bachmani*

This stocky black shorebird is a year-round resident of rugged, rocky coastlines along the entire Pacific coast, where it is surprisingly hard to see against dark rocks. The bird is often easier to locate by its loud call. Like its East Coast counterpart, the American Oystercatcher, its bill is laterally compressed at the tip, sharp and chisel-like. The Black Oystercatcher makes a living prying mollusks such as mussels and limpets off the rocks as they are exposed by the falling tide.

Identification 17–19". Large, stocky. Adult is entirely black with long, bright red bill; yellow eyes; and somewhat short, thick, pink legs. Immature is browner than adult; bill orange with dusky tip. Only other black shorebird in range is Black Turnstone, which has short, dark bill and white at base of tail, in wings, and on belly.

Voice A loud, ringing *wheep*, often uttered in series.

Habitat Rocky shores. Rarely sand or mudflats.

Range Year-round resident on the West Coast from western Aleutian Islands south to California.

106

American Avocet *Recurvirostra americana*

The avocet's genus name refers to the bird's peculiar, upturned bill by which it is easily identified. It uses its odd bill to stir aquatic insects and their larvae from the bottom of shallow pools as it feeds in unison, side by side, with others of its species. Of the world's four avocets, the American Avocet is the only representative in North America.

Identification | 17–18½". Large, boldly patterned shorebird with very long blue-gray legs and a long, slender, strongly upturned bill. Black-and-white back and wings are offset by white underparts. Head and neck are bright rusty orange in breeding plumage, gray in winter.

Voice | A loud *pleek* or *kleep, kleep.*

Habitat | Wet meadows and pastures with shallow pools, alkali ponds; also saltwater and freshwater marshes.

Range | Breeds in the West from Alberta to Manitoba and south throughout the western U.S. to Texas; in the East, coastally from New Jersey to Georgia. Winters in coastal California, Florida, and Georgia, and along the Gulf Coast.

Greater Yellowlegs *Tringa melanoleuca*

This and its close relative the Lesser Yellowlegs are included in a group of shorebirds often referred to as "tattlers." Gunners during the turn of the century used this name for shorebirds that sound an alarm when approached too closely. This alerts all birds in the area and is often followed by a swift departure of the entire flock.

Identification   13". Note the long yellow legs; plumage is salt and pepper gray above, white below, variably flecked or barred with black; overall appearance is quite dark at times, particularly in breeding plumage. Compared with Lesser Yellowlegs, bill proportionally longer and heavier with a very slight upturn.

Voice   A emphatic three-noted whistle, *tu-tu-tu*, the last note slightly lower.

Habitat   Nests in boggy boreal forests and adjacent tundra. During migration and winter, in mudflats, salt marshes, grassy freshwater marshes, and shores of ponds, lakes, and rivers.

Range   Breeds from southern Alaska east to Newfoundland. Winters along the Atlantic coast north to Long Island, Pacific coast north to Washington, and along Gulf Coast.

Willet *Catoptrophorus semipalmatus*

In the winter, the Willet is commonly seen strolling along sand beaches in the southern United States, feeding at the edge of the water. At rest, this large grayish sandpiper looks rather like a Greater Yellowlegs, in flight its bold black-and-white wing pattern is virtually unmistakable. Also, as it flies it frequently utters its name-saying call.

Identification 14–16½". Large, long-legged sandpiper with fairly heavy, long, straight, dark bill. Breeding plumage is dark brownish gray, heavily spotted and barred overall. Winter plumage is medium to pale gray above, white below. Legs are bluish gray.

Voice A repeated, rolling *will-will-willet*. Also a noisy, shrill *kreer-reer-reerr*.

Habitat In West, in wet fields, prairies, marshes, and along lakeshores. In East, primarily in salt marsh.

Range Breeds inland from Alberta to Nevada and Minnesota; coastally from Nova Scotia to Florida and to Texas. Winters along Pacific from Oregon to Baja, and along the Atlantic north to Virginia.

112

Wandering Tattler *Heteroscelus incanus*

The Wandering Tattler is most frequently encountered singly along exposed rocky shores on the West Coast. Though not closely related, this sandpiper and the Surfbird are ecologically similar: They occupy the same types of winter habitats, have same winter range, and breed in similar remote areas. The tattler's habit of "teetering" its head and tail is similar to Spotted Sandpiper.

Identification 11". Breeding plumage is dark slate-gray above, white below with heavy black barring. Winter plumage is similar but lacking barring on underparts. Medium length, straight bill is all dark. Legs are dull greenish yellow. In flight is told from other shorebirds by entirely dark upperparts.

Voice A series of rapid, high-pitched whistles, *teedle-dee, teedle-dee, teedle-dee.*

Habitat Breeds along mountain streams; winters along rocky shores; rarely on sandy beaches and mudflats.

Range Breeds in interior from western Alaska east to Yukon and south to northwestern British Columbia. Winters along Pacific coast from central California south.

114

Spotted Sandpiper *Actitis macularia*

The Spotted Sandpiper is one of the few species in its family that nests throughout most of the contiguous 48 states. Simple grass-lined depressions on the ground, the nests are usually well hidden in vegetation surrounding wetlands. Spotted Sandpipers sometimes nest in loosely formed colonies. During the winter months some can be found along the Gulf Coast, but the majority go farther south to Central and South America.

Identification 7½". A medium-size sandpiper. Most easily recognized by its teetering or bobbing habit. Breeding plumage is heavily spotted below and brownish gray above. Winter plumage lacks spots. In flight, note the white line extending lengthwise down the wing; also a low flight with a few quick shallow flaps alternating with short glides on down-bowed wings.

Voice Clear, whistled *peet-weet!;* also *weet, weet, weet.*

Habitat Shorelines.

Range Breeds throughout most of North America, except southernmost U.S., where it winters.

116

Whimbrel *Numenius phaeopus*

The Whimbrel is a curlew, a group of sandpipers that have largely brown plumage and a long, slender, down-curved bill. Whimbrels insert their long bill into the deep burrows of fiddler crabs, grasping a quarry few other birds can reach. Whimbrels utter an easily imitated whistle that may be used to lure them within close viewing range.

Identification 15–18". A large sandpiper, brown above, paler below with a long, slender, down-curved bill. Note the distinctive black and white head stripes.

Voice A rapid series of whistled notes on one pitch: *whi whi whi whi whi,* or *pip pip pip pip.*

Habitat Nests on tundra; seen in migration and in winter on a variety of coastal habitats including salt marshes, mudflats, and beaches; also inland along lakeshores, or in wet fields.

Range Breeds in northern Alaska, northwestern Canada, and along western shore of Hudson Bay. Winters along all three coasts from southern Oregon and North Carolina south.

118

Long-billed Curlew *Numenius americanus*

The Long-billed Curlew represents one end of the spectrum of sandpiper bill shapes. Extraordinarily long and decurved, its bill is used to probe into soft earth and mud to depths unattainable by other species. This assures that the Long-billed's food source will be uncontested by competitors.

Identification	20–26". One of largest shorebirds in the world. Exceptionally long, down-curved bill. Warm, speckled brown above, paler buff brown below. Note lack of crown stripes and, in flight, the cinnamon-colored underwing.
Voice	A clear, two-noted whistle, the second note on a higher pitch than the first: *cur-lee?* Also, a very rapid *wit-wit-wit-wit-wit.*
Habitat	Nests on upland prairies and grasslands; in winter, frequents a variety of wetlands including salt marshes, mudflats, and beaches.
Range	Breeds from southern British Columbia east to Manitoba and south to California and the Texas panhandle. Winters in California, southwestern Arizona; also central Texas south to the Gulf Coast and east to Louisiana.

Marbled Godwit *Limosa fedoa*

This very large sandpiper breeds in the short-grass prairies of the central plains. If not for its bill shape, it could be easily mistaken for a Long-billed Curlew, which shares its habitat and part of its range. Like the curlew's, the godwit's bill is, proportionally, one of the longest of any species of bird in North America, and it uses it to probe deep into soft earth and mud for worms and other invertebrates.

Identification 16–20". Very large shorebird. Rich buff-brown, mottled above, barred below. Winter plumage and immature are slightly paler and less barred below. Bill is extremely long, slender, and slightly upturned; pink with black tip.

Voice Especially noisy on breeding grounds; a repeated *ker-rek* or *godwit* with emphasis on the second syllable.

Habitat Breeds in wet meadows and prairies; winters along seashores on tidal flats and beaches.

Range Breeds from central Alberta to eastern Manitoba, south to Montana, South Dakota, and Minnesota. Winters on all three coasts from Oregon and Virginia south.

Ruddy Turnstone *Arenaria interpres*

This striking sandpiper is often found on rocky shores with other shorebirds such as the Purple Sandpiper on the East Coast or Black Turnstone and Surfbird on the West Coast. Ruddy Turnstones use their short bill to pry small shellfish off rocks or to flip stones (hence the name) and shells in search of invertebrates. On beaches they forage in the sand, using their bill as a spade to dig holes. Sometimes the holes become so deep the birds disappear from sight and the only evidence of their presence is the occasional spray of sand out the top as the bird continues its excavation.

Identification   8–10". Breeding plumage is bright rusty red and black on the wings and back; black-and-white head; and white underparts with bold black bib across breast. Short bill. Rather short, coral red legs. Winter plumage is duller.

Voice   A low, guttural rattle; also a low *cut-a-cut*.

Habitat   Most commonly on rocky shores and sandy beaches; less frequently in fields, dunes, and marshes.

Range   Breeds in the high Arctic. Winters along all three coasts from Oregon and Massachusetts south.

Black Turnstone *Arenaria melanocephala*

This sandpiper and its close relative the Ruddy Turnstone derive their common names from their habit of flipping stones and debris in search of small invertebrates on which they feed. They are most frequently found in small flocks on rocky shorelines, inhabiting similar areas as Black Oystercatchers and Surfbirds. Black Turnstones are less inclined than Ruddy Turnstones to forage on sand beaches.

Identification 9". Medium-size shorebird, with rather short, dark legs. Short, stout bill with upward bevel to lower mandible. In flight, has very conspicuous flash of white at base of tail and on wings. Breeding plumage, blackish above and on breast; white belly; small white spot on face at base of bill. In winter plumage, a dark portion of the plumage is dark brown; lacks the white facial spot.

Voice A grating rattle; *kr-re-e-e-r.*

Habitat Coastal marshy tundra during breeding season; in winter, along seaweed-strewn rocky shores.

Range Breeds in coastal Alaska. Winters along the entire Pacific coast from southeastern Alaska southward.

126

Surfbird *Aphriza virgata*

Surfbirds nest far inland on alpine tundra, in the mountains of interior Alaska, while in the fall and winter they are strictly coastal. Because these sandpipers nest in such remote areas, the location of their breeding grounds remained a mystery until 1921, when a pair with young was discovered in Denali National Park. Relatives of turnstones, Surfbirds are often seen foraging with their smaller cousins.

Identification 10". Fairly large, stocky sandpiper with rather short, thick, yellowish-green legs. Black bill is short and thick, orange at base. Breeding plumage has upperparts strongly speckled gray and black, scapulars rusty red; underparts mostly white with heavy black streaks. In winter plumage, dark gray above and on breast, mostly white below. In flight, told from turnstones by lack of white in back.

Voice A low *kee-wee.*

Habitat Breeds above timberline on alpine tundra; winters on rocky shores, islets, rarely on sandy beaches.

Range Breeds in interior Alaska and western Yukon; winters along Pacific from southeastern Alaska to Baja California.

Western Sandpiper *Calidris mauri*

This tiny sandpiper belongs to a group known as "peeps" because of their high, thin call notes. All five North American species are similar in general appearance. The Western Sandpiper is the most abundant in the West while the Semipalmated is most common in the East.

Identification 6–7". Very similar to others in *Calidris* genus. Particular attention should be given to precise shape of bill when attempting to separate the species. Black bill of Western is longer with slight droop at tapered tip than others. Black legs. Breeding plumage is brown and rusty-red above with conspicuous dark streaks on white breast and flanks; white belly. Paler, grayer in fall and winter.

Voice Flight call a high, thin *jeet*.

Habitat Breeds on tundra; in migration, prefers saltwater mudflats, lagoons, and ponds.

Range Breeds in northern and western coastal Alaska. In migration, primarily in the western half of continent especially on coast. Winters on coasts from Washington and Delaware south.

Sanderling *Calidris alba*

This quintessential sandpiper resembles a small wind-up toy as it "plays tag" with waves at the beach. In actuality these birds are foraging for small invertebrates in the sand at the tide line. They scurry down the beach as a wave recedes, probe repeatedly with a rapid stabbing motion, then quickly retreat back up the beach as the next wave washes over the sand. The Sanderling is a hardy species that remains on northern beaches throughout the winter.

Identification 7–8½". Small with black legs and medium-length black bill. Breeding plumage is bright rusty-red head, back, wings, and breast; white belly. Winter plumage is pale speckled gray above, white below. In flight, note the conspicuous white stripe extending down length of wing.

Voice A sharp, distinctive *kip* or *kit*, given singly or in a series.

Habitat Nests on dry, stony tundra; winters on sandy beaches and tidal flats.

Range Breeds in high Arctic tundra from Alaska eastward to Baffin Island; winters along coasts from Alaska and Nova Scotia southward.

132

Purple Sandpiper *Calidris maritima*

Ranging as far as Labrador and Newfoundland, the Purple Sandpiper winters farther north than any other Eastern sandpiper. And unlike most sandpipers in its range, in winter it is found almost exclusively on rugged, rocky shores. Purples typically feed at the edge of the water as the tide recedes, picking among the rocks as they forage for small marine invertebrates. Their stout legs and feet are well adapted to gripping even as surf washes over the rocks.

Identification 8–9½". Fairly stocky with medium-length bill, orange at the base, darkening toward slightly drooped tip. Dull orange legs. Breeding plumage, speckled dark brown and black above; light brown breast lightly streaked; white flanks boldly streaked; white belly. Winter plumage, dark purplish-gray back, head, and breast; white below with dark streaks.

Voice Twitters, trills; in flight, issues a soft *prrt-prrt*.

Habitat Breeds on tundra and gravel barrens. In winter, is on rocky coasts, including breakwaters.

Range Breeds in high Arctic. Winters on Atlantic coast from Newfoundland to Virginia.

134

Dunlin *Calidris alpina*

The name Dunlin refers to this sandpiper's dull gray winter plumage. Previously it was called the Red-backed Sandpiper for its bright rusty back in breeding plumage. This is one of the few sandpipers that spends the winter in the North Temperate Zone, and is usually found in large foraging flocks feeding on a wide variety of coastal invertebrates such as small mollusks and worms.

Identification 7½–9". Black bill, long with a pronounced droop at tip. Breeding plumage, upperparts, especially back, rusty red; underparts white with fine black streaks on breast, and black belly-patch. Winter plumage, upperparts uniform medium gray, underparts pale gray to whitish.

Voice A distinctive harsh *jeerp;* a soft *chu* when taking flight.

Habitat Breeds on tundra. Winters on beaches and tidal flats. Generally prefers to feed in mud, but forages on substrates including jetties; also found inland during migration.

Range Breeds in northern Alaska and Canada south to James Bay. Winters along all coasts from southern Alaska and Massachusetts to Mexico.

Long-billed Dowitcher *Limnodromus scolopaceus*

Because of their very similar appearance, the two North American dowitchers—the Long-billed and Short-billed—were not recognized as distinct species until the 1950s. The Long-billed, like other Dowitchers, feeds by rapidly probing its bill vertically into mud.

Identification 10½–12". Very long, straight bill. Rather heavy body and relatively short legs impart somewhat dumpy appearance. Breeding plumage is dark speckled brown above, rusty-orange below, with spotting and barring. Winter plumage is cold gray above, mostly white below. In flight, white wedge extends up onto lower back between wings.

Voice A short, high *keek*. Short-billed gives a fluty, rapidly whistled *tu-tu-tu*).

Habitat In migration, most widespread dowitcher in interior, where it shows preference for edges of ponds, lakes, and marshes. More coastal in winter.

Range Breeds in northern Alaska , adjacent Yukon and northwest territories. Winters in coastal states from Washington and Virginia south. Also in southern Arizona and New Mexico.

Red-necked Phalarope *Phalaropus lobatus*

The Red-necked Phalarope and its close relative the Red Phalarope are the only oceanic sandpipers. They and the Wilson's Phalarope are unusual among birds in being polyandrous—that is, the larger and more colorful female mates with and lays egg clutches for two or more males, each of which is then left to incubate and care for young.

Identification 7". Breeding plumage in female generally dark above with rusty red on neck; white throat and underparts. Male is similar but much duller. In winter, sexes essentially similar: dark gray back and wings, hindneck, and hindcrown; white elsewhere except for black eye-patch. Very similar to winter plumaged Red Phalarope but, at close range, note the Red-necked's darker back and thinner bill.

Voice A clipped *kip*, sometimes given in a series.

Habitat Breeds on wet, arctic tundra; winters at sea in Southern Hemisphere.

Range Breeds in Alaska and across northern Canada; may be seen in migration off both coasts, more commonly in the West, where it also occasionally occurs inland.

140

Parasitic Jaeger *Stercorarius parasiticus*

All three species of jaeger—the Pomarine, Parasitic, and Long-tailed—nest in arctic tundra but spend most of the year at sea. Swift and powerful flyers, jaegers either capture live prey such as small rodents or birds, or harass other seabirds into relinquishing their catch. Parasitic Jaegers may be the most proficient, often pursuing their victims in pairs or teams. In breeding plumage, jaegers possess a characteristically shaped pair of central tail feathers, which aid in identification.

Identification	18". Medium-size, falcon-shape seabird with long pointed wings. Highly variable plumage from pale tan to nearly black. In breeding plumage the two pointed central tail feathers are elongated into a spike.
Voice	On breeding grounds, utters a wailing cry, *ka-aaow* or *ya-wow.*
Habitat	Nests on wet tundra; or open ocean the rest of the year.
Range	Breeds from Alaska to north-central Canada. Migrates off both coasts.

Laughing Gull *Larus atricilla*

The Laughing Gull is the most common and widespread gull along the southern Atlantic and Gulf coasts. The adult in breeding plumage is easily recognizable by its distinctive black hood, and by its characteristic, high-pitched, laughing cry. Highly opportunistic, like most gulls, the Laughing Gull has become expert in stealing a meal from a Brown Pelican, landing on the head of the pelican and snatching the food directly from the pelican's bill.

Identification
16–17". Breeding plumage is dark gray back and wings; black hood; white underparts and tail; bill deep red. Winter plumage is similar but black hood reduced to smudgy gray nape; bill blackish. Immature is brown (molting to dark gray) above with brown wing coverts and pale head and underparts. Broad black band on tip of tail. Legs are black.

Voice
A nasal, high *ca-ha*, sometimes extended *ha-ha-haah-haah-haah.*

Habitat
Seacoasts, salt marshes, bays, beaches; rare inland.

Range
Nests coastally from Maine to Texas. Retreats from northernmost part of its breeding range in winter.

Bonaparte's Gull *Larus philadelphia*

Because of its light, buoyant flight and delicate build, this attractive little gull more closely resembles a tern than a gull. In winter, Bonaparte's Gulls are often found in large, cohesive flocks deftly dodging breakers off beaches or foraging over rips at river mouths and sewage outfalls. Bonaparte's Gull is the only North American gull that nests in trees.

Identification 12–14". Small. Mostly white with pale gray back. Upper wing pale gray with a large white triangle on the leading edge of primaries, and narrow band of black on trailing edge of primaries. Black hood in breeding plumage. White head with blackish spot behind eye in winter plumage.

Voice A rasping *tea-ar;* also a nasal snarl.

Habitat Breeds in northern coniferous forests along lakes and rivers; winters along coast and on waterways.

Range Breeds from Alaska, through most of Canada south of the treeline, southeast to James Bay. Winters on all three coasts from Washington and New Brunswick south, and on the Great Lakes.

Heermann's Gull *Larus heermanni*

This elegant and distinctive gull does not nest north of Mexico, but disperses north following the breeding cycle. It is one of few species of North American birds that winters north of its breeding grounds. Heermann's Gull nests colonially in desert habitat and faces the unusual problem of having to incubate its eggs to keep them cool rather than warm. This bird was named in 1852 for nineteenth-century field ornithologist Dr. Adolphus Heermann.

Identification 16½–18½". Breeding plumage is uniformly gray body with contrasting white head, unique among North American gulls; black tail with narrow white band at tip; bill is bright red. Immature is dark sooty brown overall with a bicolored bill. Attains adult plumage in third year. Could be confused with a dark jaeger, but lacks white in the primaries.

Voice A nasal, whiny *see-whee;* also a low-pitched *kuk-kuk-kuk.*

Habitat Coastal waters and beaches.

Range Summer and fall visitor along Pacific coast as far north as Puget Sound; remains through winter as far north as San Francisco.

148

Ring-billed Gull *Larus delawarensis*

The Ring-billed Gull, although common on the coasts especially during winter, is regularly found inland and typically nests in freshwater habitats. They are often found at landfills, shopping malls, and around fast-food restaurants. The Ring-Billed is called a three-year gull because it takes three years to attain adult plumage through a series of biannual molts.

Identification   18–21". Adult has a white head and underparts with a gray back; black-and-white tipped gray wings. Note the yellowish legs, eye, and bill with a black ring near tip. Young birds are overall gray and brown with a dark bill and grayish legs.

Voice   A high, shrill *ky-eow.*

Habitat   Nests on islands or shores of inland lakes and marshes; during migration and winter, in landfills, wet fields, and on lakes, rivers, and seashores.

Range   Widely dispersed throughout prairies of Canada and the U.S.,Washington and Oregon, and the Great Lakes region. Winters along coast north to British Columbia in the west, Nova Scotia in the east, and as far inland as Kansas.

California Gull *Larus californicus*

Like the Ring-billed Gull, the California Gull is regularly found inland during breeding season. Also like the Ring-billed, insects form an important part of its diet. In fact, the California Gull is celebrated as something of a protector in the Mormon tradition, as these gulls eliminated large numbers of locusts that threatened the early settlers' crops.

Identification 23–29". Very similar to Herring Gull. In summer, the breeding ranges of the two species may be helpful in differentiating the species. Generally the California Gull is smaller than the Herring Gull. In adult plumage, its gray back and wings are slightly darker, and the bill is slimmer. Also note the dark eye, the black and red spots near the tip of the yellow bill, and the yellowish-green legs.

Voice A repeated *kee-yah.*

Habitat Inland lakes and marshes; winters along coast.

Range Alberta and Saskatchewan south to Wyoming and Utah, and west to California. Winters along Pacific coast.

Herring Gull *Larus argentatus*

The quintessential sea gull found virtually throughout the Northern Hemisphere, the Herring Gull has learned to exploit a wide variety of foods and habitats. However, its appearance as a breeding bird in much of the United States occurred relatively recently, and coincided with sudden curtailment of widespread hunting and increases in use of landfills and large-scale commercial fisheries.

Identification 23–26". Adult plumage, pale gray back and upper wings; black and white wingtips; pure white elsewhere. Bill is yellow with red spot, legs pale flesh-colored. Immature is mottled brown, attaining adult plumage by fourth year.

Voice A squealing *ke-yah, ke-ya;* also *eeeyou.*

Habitat Virtually anywhere within striking range of water. Occasionally nests on flat rooftops and in landfills.

Range Breeds from Alaska east through northern Canada to Newfoundland, south to the Great Lakes and along East coast to South Carolina. Winters from southeastern Alaska, Columbia, Washington, and Colorado, east to the Great Lakes and Newfoundland, south to Mexico.

Western Gull *Larus occidentalis*

This large, dark gull is found almost exclusively along the West Coast of the United States. Within that range, it is the only dark-backed gull (excluding vagrants), and therefore is not likely to be confused with any other species. However, the Western Gull does frequently interbreed with the equally common Glaucous-winged Gull, and identification of these hybrids is difficult at best.

Identification 20–23". A large, heavy-bodied gull. Adult plumage, dark gray back and wings (darkest at southern end of range, lightening slightly northward), with black-and-white tips to primaries; white head, tail and underparts; dull pink legs; heavy bill, yellow with red spot near tip. Immature is dark mottled brown; attains adult plumage by fourth year.

Voice Loud, squealing calls, *keeoh, keeoh, keeoh.* Also a nasal *ha ha ha ha.*

Habitat A variety of coastal habitats including coastal landfills and open ocean, out to about 70 miles.

Range Resident on Pacific coast from Washington south to Baja California.

156

Glaucous-winged Gull *Larus glaucescens*

The Glaucous-winged Gull is one of the most frequently encountered gulls of the Pacific Northwest. It shares part of its range with the Western Gull and the species frequently interbreed to produce various hybrid offspring. To further confuse the issue, the Glaucous-winged also hybridizes with other similar species in its range, including Herring and Glaucous gulls.

Identification 21–24". Compared to the Herring Gull, slightly larger, heavier-billed, and paler on the back and wings. Wing tips are frosted with variable shades of gray. Eye is dark.

Voice A raucous series of notes on one pitch.

Habitat Seacoasts and open seas; harbors, landfills and fish canneries; rarely inland, except in broad river valleys of the Northwest.

Range Resident from Aleutian Islands and western and southern coasts of Alaska south to northwestern Washington. In winter, south along Pacific coast to Baja California.

Great Black-backed Gull *Larus marinus*

The Great Black-backed Gull is the largest gull in the world, and it uses its size to full advantage. While gulls are generally thought of as rather benign, the Black-backed is an aggressive and voracious predator at the top of the food chain. It rarely misses an opportunity to snatch an unguarded egg or chick from a nest, and occasionally, even seemingly healthy adult birds may be savaged by a marauding Black-backed.

Identification   28–31". Nearly goose-size. Adult has black back and upper wings, elsewhere white; heavy bill, yellow with red spot. Immature is speckled dark brown and white on back and wings with paler head and underparts; bill is mostly black; attains adult plumage in fourth year.

Voice   A deep, guttural *keeow.*

Habitat   Seacoasts. Also landfills and less commonly on inland lakes and rivers.

Range   Breeds along the Atlantic Coast from Labrador south to North Carolina and inland to Great Lakes. Winters south to Florida.

160

Black-legged Kittiwake *Rissa tridactyla*

This small gull nests on narrow cliff ledges in enormous colonies on the sea. One of the few cliff-nesting gulls, the kittiwake has developed several space-saving adaptations for life on the edge. For example, whereas ground-nesting gulls lay an average of three eggs, kittiwakes lay only two. The bird is named for its ringing, name-saying cry.

Identification 17". Adult in breeding plumage has upper wings and back gray; wing tips pure black, as if dipped in ink; head, tail, and underparts white; bill greenish yellow. Winter adult, gray smudge on back of head. Immature has upperwing with blackish bar extending from tips of wings inward along leading edge of primaries, and across center of inner portion of wing (thus forming a flattened W or M). Black collar on nape and black band at tip of tail. Legs are black.

Voice An oft-repeated, high-pitched *kitti-wake, kitti-wake.*

Habitat Breeds on seaside cliffs; winters at sea.

Range Breeds throughout coastal Alaska, Northwest Territories, and Canadian Maritimes. Winters from Alaska to California, and from Newfoundland to the Gulf of Mexico.

Royal Tern *Sterna maxima*

This is the second largest tern in North America, the Caspian Tern being the only species larger. The Royal is primarily a southern species, a familiar sight along shores in the southern Atlantic and Gulf states, where it is often found resting on a convenient perch such as a buoy or piling. Unlike the Caspian, they occur only on salt water. Royals breed in very large colonies.

Identification 18–21". In breeding plumage, has pale gray upper wings and back; black cap with shaggy crest on back of head; rest of plumage white; bill is bright orange, large; legs are black, very short. Nonbreeding plumage is similar except forecrown is white. The similar Caspian Tern has a thicker, blood-red bill and, in flight, more black in primaries.

Voice A raspy, high-pitched *kree-er,* or *kak.*

Habitat Saltwater habitats; nests on sheltered, sandy beaches.

Range Breeds along Gulf of Mexico from Texas to northern Florida, and on Atlantic Coast from central Florida north to Maryland. Winters from Virginia south to Florida and west to Texas, and in southern California.

164

Arctic Tern *Sterna paradisaea*

The Arctic Tern is the champion of all migrants. Following its breeding season in the Arctic, it engages in a migration that takes it to the waters off Antarctica—a round-trip, annual journey of over 20,000 miles! This schedule allows the Arctic Tern to enjoy more daylight hours than any other creature in the world.

Identification 14–17". Slender with long, pointed, angular wings and a long, deeply forked tail. Pale gray back and upper wing, light gray underparts contrasting with a white cheek, black cap (breeding plumage), and white tail. At close range, compared with more widespread Common Tern, note clear, silvery upper surface of primaries in flight, and shorter, entirely red bill (tip of Common's bill is black).

Voice A descending, raspy *kee-ar.* Also a repeated *kee-kee-kee-kee.*

Habitat Northern lakes, ponds, rivers, and seacoasts.

Range Breeds throughout Arctic south to southeastern Alaska in the West and Massachusetts in the East. Winters in Antarctic seas.

166

Forster's Tern *Sterna forsteri*

As with all tern species, Forster's is normally found near water. Marshes, estuaries, and coastal beaches are its favorite haunts. And while Forster's obtains some of its food in typical tern fashion, diving into the water for small fish, it is also adept at catching flying insects. These birds are regularly observed sweeping low over marsh vegetation in search of dragonflies, damselflies, and other insects.

Identification 14–16¼". Breeding plumage has a black cap and nape, gray upperparts, deeply forked tail, and reddish legs and bill. Note the frosty look to the upperwings and the white underparts. In winter adult and immature plumage, the bill is black and the black head markings are reduced to an area forming an eyepatch.

Voice A raspy, buzzy *zraa* or *zrurr.* Also shrill *pip-pip,* or *kit, kit, kit.*

Habitat Inland and coastal marshes and seacoasts.

Range Breeds from Canadian prairies to Colorado and California; also on the mid-Atlantic coast. Winters along southeastern and Gulf coasts, and southern California coast.

168

Least Tern *Sterna antillarum*

Our smallest tern species, the Least Tern is found coastally and inland. A threatened species over much of its North American breeding range, the Least Tern is adversely affected by human intrusions into its nesting colonies. Like many species, the Least Tern may abandon its nest if disturbed. Effective conservation measures, including fences and signs, provide protection at some colonies.

Identification 8½–9½". Small. Gray above and white below. In breeding plumage, note the black cap, white forehead, and delicate yellow bill.

Voice Repeated, somewhat tinny, two-syllable *kachink*. Also a sharp *kit, kit*.

Habitat Beaches and sandbars along shallow rivers and lakes, and seacoasts.

Range Breeds along the Pacific coast north to roughly San Francisco, along the Atlantic coast north to Maine, and inland along the largest rivers.

Black Skimmer *Rynchops niger*

This highly distinctive, gull-like bird possesses a remarkable bill, laterally compressed with a sharp, chisel-like tip and with the lower mandible substantially longer than the upper. Only skimmers possess this unique bill design. While feeding, skimmers fly low over the water, dipping their longer lower mandible into the water and skimming the surface for small fish and other animals. When they hit a fish, the bill snaps shut.

Identification	16–20". Unmistakable. Long, narrow wings and uniquely shaped, bright red bill with black tip (see above). Adult, black above, white below. Immature is scaly brown above and white below.
Voice	A short, soft *yap*; also soft cooing on breeding grounds.
Habitat	Prefers saltwater habitats such as sandy beaches, shallow bays, and estuaries, but the bird can also be found inland on large rivers and lakes.
Range	Breeds from Massachusetts south to Florida and along the Gulf Coast to Texas, and south from southern California. Retreats from northernmost breeding range in winter.

172

Common Murre *Uria aalge*

Except for the fact that these black-and-white seabirds can fly, Common Murres are quite similar to penguins. Penguins, however, are SouthernHemisphere birds while alcids—the family to which murres and puffins belong—are exclusively in the Northern Hemisphere. Unfortunately, murres are threatened by the continued use of illegal drift nets by commercial fishermen. The birds dive under water for fish and become entangled in these nets and drown.

Identification 16–17". Sturdy, ducklike seabirds with rather narrow, pointed bills. Breeding plumage, back, head, and breast black. Winter plumage, black on head only as far down as eye; rest of underparts white. Very similar and less common Thick-billed Murre shows a thin white streak on the bill.

Voice Purring or murmur, from which the name is derived.

Habitat Breeds in large colonies on steep coastal cliffs. Winters at sea.

Range Breeds from Alaska south to central California, and in the East in Newfoundland and Nova Scotia. Winters to southern California, and on Atlantic to Long Island.

174

Black Guillemot *Cepphus grylle*

This sleekly beautiful seabird and its West Coast counterpart, the Pigeon Guillemot, differ from most members of their family in being almost entirely black in breeding plumage, and by remaining close to shore near their coastal nesting colonies throughout the winter rather than migrating offshore. They do, however, share the alcid habit of "flying" under water in pursuit of fish.

Identification 13". Breeding plumage, entirely black except for a white wing patch that is clearly visible both at rest and in flight. In winter, salt-and-pepper plumage appears whitish. Immature is slightly browner than winter adult. Pigeon Guillemot is identical to Black except for a small black wedge through the white wing-patch.

Voice A shrill *squeee*.

Habitat Breeds on rocky, coastal cliffs. Winters in coastal waters.

Range Breeds from Arctic Canada south to Canadian Maritimes, Maine, and New Hampshire; also northern Alaska. Winters on the Atlantic south to Rhode Island. Alaskan population winters in the Arctic Sea.

176

Tufted Puffin *Fratercula cirrhata*

Like its two relatives, the Atlantic and Horned puffins, the Tufted Puffin has a huge, laterally flattened, brightly colored bill. Puffins are compact seabirds that nest colonially (each pair in its own burrow), and otherwise spend the rest of the year fishing at sea. The Tufted Puffin is, marginally, the largest of the three species of puffins in the world. It ranges farther south than either the Horned or the Atlantic puffins.

Identification	15–16". Adult in breeding plumage is unmistakable: huge, pale yellow and reddish-orange bill; black body; head black except for white face and distinctive straw-yellow plumes (or "tufts") extending back from behind the eyes. Winter plumage, bill is smaller, duller; lacks plumes. Told from other puffins by its dark underparts.
Voice	Usually silent, growling sounds around nest site.
Habitat	Nests on islands in cliff-top burrows, on sea slopes, or in rock crevices. Winters at sea.
Range	Breeds from northwestern Alaska along coast to central California. Winters at sea throughout the North Pacific.

178

Atlantic Puffin *Fratercula arctica*

The Atlantic Puffin is also known as the "Sea Parrot," a name that alludes to the adult's large, multicolored bill. It is highly skilled at "flying" under water in pursuit of fish. According to some ornithologists, puffins defy the laws of aerodynamics by achieving aerial flight despite their disproportionally tiny wings. The Horned Puffin is the Pacific look-alike.

Identification   12–13". Compact body, black above and white below. Black collar extends from upperparts across throat. Face is white in summer, gray in winter. Grotesquely large, laterally compressed bill is banded with orange; yellow and bluish in summer, duller in winter. Bill of immature is narrower, duller. Legs are bright reddish orange.

Voice   Deep, throaty purrs and a single growl.

Habitat   Nests in burrows on coastal islands; otherwise at sea.

Range   Breeds on the Atlantic coast from Labrador and Newfoundland south to Maine. Winters far out at sea, east of its colonies, and less commonly south to waters off Massachusetts.

Belted Kingfisher *Ceryle alcyon*

The Belted Kingfisher is often seen along the edges of ponds, lakes, rivers, and estuaries throughout much of North America. A rattled flight call is often the first sign of its presence. With patience the observer will soon discover one or more of the kingfisher's favored perches from which the bird flies out to hover over the water and ultimately dive for fish. The female of this species is unusual in that she is the more colorful. Also unusual is the Belted Kingfisher's nest site, which is made at the end of a tunnel, typically excavated in a sandy bank.

Identification 11–14½". A large-headed, bushy-crested bird with a large bill. Generally slate-blue above and white below. Note the broad blue band on the upper breast; female has an additional rust-colored band on the belly. Legs are very short.

Voice In flight, a loud, prolonged rattle.

Habitat Banks of lakes, rivers, and quiet coastal lagoons and estuaries.

Range Widespread in North America.

Parts of a Bird

nape

back

scapulars

wing coverts

secondaries

primaries

tail

undertail coverts

crown

forehead

upper mandible

lower mandible

chin

throat

breast

flank

belly

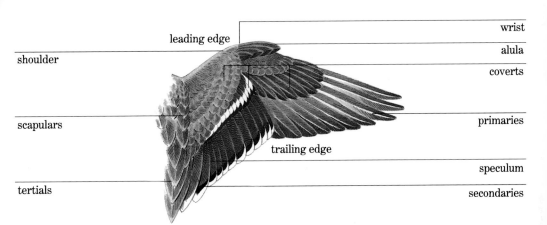

wrist

leading edge

shoulder

alula

coverts

scapulars

primaries

trailing edge

speculum

tertials

secondaries

Glossary

Alula
Small group of short feathers at the leading edge of wrist on wing.

Barred
Having lines in plumage oriented across axis of body.

Belly
Area of underparts around legs, below breast and above undertail coverts.

Cap
Contrasting color on crown (see Greater Shearwater).

Circumpolar
Occurring throughout polar regions of the world.

Coverts
Small feathers covering the leading half of the wings (wing coverts), and spanning the area between the body and the tail (tail coverts).

Crest
Erect crown and/or nape feathers.

Crown
Top of head between nape and bill.

Diurnal
Active during the day.

Flight feathers
Primaries and secondaries.

Forehead
Area on front of crown above the bill.

Immature
Nonadult.

Juvenile
Young bird in first or second plumage of its life.

Marine
Occurring in or on the surface of the ocean.

Morph
One of two or more plumage types, occurring independently of age, sex, or season.

Nape
Back of the head including the hindneck.

Nocturnal
Active during the night.

Primaries
Longest, outermost feathers of wing.

Scapulars
Several rows of feathers spanning between each wing and back.

Secondaries
Long, broad, innermost feathers forming trailing edge of wing.

Speculum
A colorful panel in the inner secondaries of some ducks.

Underparts
Collective term for all areas of the lower surfaces of the body, including chin, throat, breast, belly, flanks, and undertail coverts.

Index

A

Actitis macularia, 116
Aechmophorus occidentalis, 32
Albatross, Black-footed, 34
American Oystercatcher, 104
Anas rubripes, 74
Aphriza virgata, 128
Ardea herodias, 58
Arenaria interpres, 124
Arenaria melanocephala, 126
Avocet, American, 108
Aythya marila, 76

B

Branta canadensis, 72
Bucephala albeola, 92
Bucephala clangula, 90
Bufflehead, 92

C

Calidris alba, 132
Calidris alpina, 136
Calidris maritima, 134
Calidris mauri, 130
Casmerodius albus, 60
Catoptrophorus semipalmatus,
112
Cepphus grylle, 176

Ceryle alcyon, 182
Charadrius melodus, 102
Charadrius semipalmatus, 100
Clangula hyemalis, 82
Cormorant, Brandt's, 52
Cormorant, Double-crested, 50
Cormorant, Great, 48
Cormorant, Pelagic, 54
Curlew, Long-billed, 120
Cygnus olor, 70

D

Diomedea nigripes, 34
Dowitcher, Long-billed, 138
Duck, American Black, 74
Duck, Harlequin, 80
Dunlin, 136

E

Egret, Great, 60
Egret, Snowy, 62
Egretta caerulea, 64
Egretta thula, 62
Egretta tricolor, 66
Eider, Common, 78

F

Fratercula arctica, 180

Fratercula cirrhata, 178
Fregata magnificens, 56
Frigatebird, Magnificent, 56
Fulmar, Northern, 36
Fulmarus glacialis, 36

G
Gannet, Northern, 44
Gavia immer, 26
Gavia stellata, 24
Godwit, Marbled, 122
Goldeneye, Common, 90
Goose, Canada, 72
Grebe, Eared, 30
Grebe, Horned, 28
Grebe, Western, 32
Guillemot, Black, 176
Gull, Bonaparte's, 146
Gull, California, 152
Gull, Glaucous-winged, 158
Gull, Great Black-backed, 160
Gull, Heermann's, 148
Gull, Herring, 154
Gull, Laughing, 144
Gull, Ring-billed, 150
Gull, Western, 156

H
Haematopus bachmani, 106
Haematopus palliatus, 104
Heron, Great Blue, 58
Heron, Little Blue, 64
Heron, Tricolored, 66
Heteroscelus incanus, 114
Histrionicus histrionicus, 80

J
Jaeger, Parasitic, 142

K
Kingfisher, Belted, 182
Kittiwake, Black-legged, 162

L
Larus argentatus, 154
Larus atricilla, 144
Larus californicus, 152
Larus delawarensis, 150
Larus glaucescens, 158
Larus heermanni, 148
Larus marinus, 160
Larus occidentalis, 156
Larus philadelphia, 146
Limnodromus scolopaceus, 138
Limosa fedoa, 122

Loon, Common, 26
Loon, Red-throated, 24

M
Melanitta fusca, 88
Melanitta nigra, 84
Melanitta perspicillata, 86
Merganser, Red-breasted, 94
Mergus serrator, 94
Morus bassanus, 44
Murre, Common, 174

N
Night-Heron, Black-crowned, 68
Numenius americanus, 120
Numenius phaeopus, 118
Nycticorax nycticorax, 68

O
Oceanites oceanicus, 42
Oldsquaw, 82
Osprey, 96
Oystercatcher, Black, 106

P
Pandion haliaetus, 96
Pelecanus occidentalis, 46
Pelican, Brown, 46

Phalacrocorax auritus, 50
Phalacrocorax carbo, 48
Phalacrocorax pelagicus, 54
Phalacrocorax penicillatus, 52
Phalarope, Red-necked, 140
Phalaropus lobatus, 140
Plover, Black-bellied, 98
Plover, Piping, 102
Plover, Semipalmated, 100
Pluvialis squatarola, 98
Podiceps auritus, 28
Podiceps nigricollis, 30
Puffin, Atlantic, 180
Puffin, Tufted, 178
Puffinus gravis, 38
Puffinus griseus, 40

R
Recurvirostra americana, 108
Rissa tridactyla, 162
Rynchops niger, 172

S
Sanderling, 132
Sandpiper, Purple, 134
Sandpiper, Spotted, 116
Sandpiper, Western, 130
Scaup, Greater, 76

Scoter, Black, 84
Scoter, Surf, 86
Scoter, White-winged, 88
Shearwater, Greater, 38
Shearwater, Sooty, 40
Skimmer, Black, 172
Somateria mollissima, 78
Stercorarius parasiticus, 142
Sterna antillarum, 170
Sterna forsteri, 168
Sterna maxima, 164
Sterna paradisaea, 166
Storm-Petrel, Wilson's, 42
Surfbird, 128
Swan, Mute, 70

T
Tattler, Wandering, 114
Tern, Arctic, 166
Tern, Forster's, 168
Tern, Least, 170
Tern, Royal, 164
Tringa melanoleuca, 110
Turnstone, Black, 126
Turnstone, Ruddy, 124

U
Uria aalge, 174

W
Whimbrel, 118
Willet, 112

Y
Yellowlegs, Greater, 110

Credits

Photographers

Robert P. Abrams (31)
Steve Bentsen (183)
Fred Bruemmer (155)
Sharon Cummings (41, 51, 133)
Rob Curtis/The Early Birder (171)

DEMBINSKY PHOTO ASSOCIATES:
Dominique Braud (97)
John Gerlach (3, 109)
Gary Meszaros (93)
Rod Planck (137)
Carl R. Sams (27)

Jon Farrar (69)
Jeff Foott (79)
Chuck Gordon (25, 29, 125, 143)
G.C. Kelley (127)
Wayne Lankinen (61)
Harold Lindstrom (45, 85, 101, 113, 123, 141, 161)
Bates Littlehales (33, 47, 55, 65, 87, 89)
Barry W. Mansell (63)
C. Allan Morgan (39, 43, 53, 57)

Arthur & Elaine Morris/Birds As Art (Front Cover, 49, 67, 73, 81, 103, 105, 107, 115, 119, 121, 129, 135, 139, 145, 149, 151, 153, 157, 165, 167, 169, 181)
James F. Parnell (175)
Rod Planck (75, 91, 163)
Betty Randall (173, 179)

ROOT RESOURCES:
Jim Flynn (83)

Johann Schumacher Design (111)
Hugh P. Smith, Jr. (131)
Frank S. Todd (159)
Tom J. Ulrich (37, 177)
Mark F. Wallner (95, 117)
Tim Zurowski (22-23, 35, 59, 71, 77, 99, 147)

Cover Photograph: Brown Pelican by Arthur & Elaine Morris/ Birds As Art
Title Page: American Avocet by John Gerlach/Dembinsky Photo Associates
Spread (p. 22-23): Royal Terns by Tim Zurowski

Illustrators

Range maps by Paul Singer
Drawings by Barry Van Dusen (184-185)
Silhouette drawings by Douglas Pratt and Paul Singer

The photographers and illustrators hold copyrights to their works.

Staff

This book was created by
Chanticleer Press.
All editorial inquiries should
be addressed to:
Chanticleer Press
568 Broadway, Suite #1005A
New York, NY 10012
(212) 941-1522

Chanticleer Press Staff
Founding Publisher:
Paul Steiner
Publisher: Andrew Stewart
Managing Editor: Edie Locke
Production Manager:
Deirdre Duggan Ventry
Assistant to the Publisher:
Kelly Beekman
Text Editor: Carole Berglie
Consultant: John Farrand, Jr.
Photo Editor: Lori J. Hogan
Designer: Sheila Ross
Research Assistant:
Debora Diggins,
Marianne Maloney

The author wishes to aknowledge
the help and cooperation
provided by Richard K. Walton.

Original series design by
Massimo Vignelli.

To purchase this book or other
National Audubon Society
illustrated nature books,
please contact:
Alfred A. Knopf, Inc.
201 East 50th Street
New York, NY 10022
(800) 733-3000